Washingt

DISASTER ALERT!

Tornado Alert!

Wendy Scavuzzo

Crabtree Publishing Company

www.crabtreebooks.com

presented by:

Crabtree Publishing Company

www.crabtreebooks.com

PMB 16A, 350 Fifth Avenue
Suite 3308
New York, NY 10118

616 Welland Avenue,
St. Catharines
Ontario, Canada
L2M 5V6

73 Lime Walk
Headington
Oxford OX3 7AD
United Kingdom

To my family, with love and gratitude, for supporting me and putting up with my tornado obsession.

Coordinating editor: Ellen Rodger

Project editor: Sean Charlebois

Copy editor: Carrie Gleason

Proofreader: Adrianna Morganelli

Designer and production coordinator: Rosie Gowsell

Art director: Rob MacGregor

Photo research: Allison Napier

Indexer: Wendy Scavuzzo

Prepress: Embassy Graphics

Printing: Worzalla Publishing Company

Consultants: Dr. Richard Cheel, Earth Sciences Department, Brock University

Photographs: Paul & Lindamarie Ambrose/Getty Images: p. 3; AP/Wide World Photos p. 23 (bottom), p. 25 (both), p. 26, p. 29 (both); Roger Archibald: p. 7 (top); Bettmann/CORBIS/MAGMA: p. 24; Ron Chapple/Getty Images: p. 15 (top); Michele/Tom Grimm/Mira.com: p. 15 (top); HUBER/ORLANDO SENTINEL/CORBIS SYGMA/MAGMA: p. 22 (top); National Oceanic and Atmospheric Administration/Department of Commerce: p. 18 (right); Alan R. Moller/Getty Images: p. 20 (top); Richard Olsenius/Getty Images: p. 8; Jim Reed/Photo Researchers Inc.: p. 7 (bottom), p. 9, p. 16, p. 17 (both), p. 19, p. 20 (bottom), p. 21 (top), p. 22 (bottom); Jim Reed/Science Photo Library: p. 23(top); Reuters/CORBIS/MAGMA: p. 21 (bottom); Royalty-Free/CORBIS/MAGMA: p. 28; Fred K. Smith/Code Red: cover; Gregory Thompson: p. 7 (middle); Jeff Vanuga/CORBIS/MAGMA: p. 5; Aneal Vohra/Mira.com: p. 27 (top); Weatherstock/Warren Faidley: p. 14 (all), p. 18 (left), p. 22 (middle); A T Willett/Getty Images: p. 15 (bottom); Jim Zuckerman/CORBIS/MAGMA: p. 4

Illustrations: Dan Pressman: pp. 10-11, p. 12, p. 13; David Wysotski: pp. 30-31.

Maps: Jim Chernishenko: p. 6 (all)

Cover: Tornadoes are violent spinning windstorms that are often accompanied by lighntning.

Title page: Most tornadoes occur in the late afternoon when some people in cities are traveling home from work.

Contents: Tornadoes will take on the color of the material they pick up.

Published by
Crabtree Publishing Company

Copyright © 2004

Cataloging-in-Publication Data

Scavuzzo, Wendy.
  Tornado alert! / Wendy Scavuzzo.
    p. cm. -- (Disaster alert!)
  Includes index.
  ISBN 0-7787-1571-X (rlb) -- ISBN 0-7787-1603-1 (pbk)
  1. Tornadoes--Juvenile literature. I. Title. II. Series.
    QC955.2.S33 2004
    551.55'3--dc22

2004000837
LC

Table of Contents

Twister!

Tornadoes are nature's most violent storms, with wind speeds that can reach 318 miles per hour (512 km/h). They can carry debris for hundreds of miles, toss railway cars, and flatten entire neighborhoods into rubble in mere seconds. Tornadoes are the third largest cause of weather-related deaths in the United States.

What is a disaster? A disaster is a destructive event that affects the natural world and human communities. Some disasters are predictable and others occur without warning. Coping successfully with a disaster depends on a community's preparation.

Explaining tornadoes

Almost everything known about tornadoes has been learned since the 1950s, when two air force **meteorologists** realized there was a connection between a type of cloud and tornadoes. In the 1970s, scientists began to use **Doppler radar** to track tornadoes. Over the years, they studied their findings and improved their equipment. Scientists now know more about tornadoes, but there is still a lot to learn. At one time, the only way people knew that a tornado was coming was because they saw or heard it. By then, it was often too late to take cover and many lives were lost. Now, meteorologists, armed with their weather knowledge and storm-tracking equipment, can forecast possible tornadoes so that people can be warned in time.

Tornado myths

At one time, Native Americans believed that some areas were protected from tornadoes by land features, such as hills, mountain, ridges, or rivers. They passed these legends on to the early settlers, who passed them down through the generations. The legends caused a false sense of security, as people later found out. Tornadoes have crossed almost every major river east of the Rocky Mountains, including the Mississippi River, and many mountains and high hills. In Topeka, Kansas, people believed that Burnett's Mound, a large landform on the southwest side of the city, was "protecting" them. In 1966, a very violent tornado tore over Burnett's Mound and right through Topeka. It killed 21 people and caused 100 million dollars in damage.

In 1987, a violent tornado crossed the Continental Divide in Yellowstone National Park.

5

What is a Tornado?

A tornado is a violent, rotating windstorm that forms from towering thunderstorms called supercells. The supercells contains air currents that move up and down at increasing speeds, until they spin into a funnel-shaped cloud. If the funnel cloud touches the ground, it becomes a tornado.

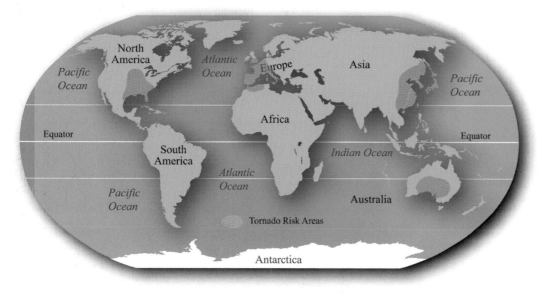

Many parts of the world experience tornadoes. In the United States, Texas averages 125 tornadoes per year. Australia and Bangladesh are also hit by several tornadoes each year.

Tornado Alley

Every state in the United States experiences tornadoes, but a wide strip of land running through the center of the country has more tornadoes every year than any other place on Earth. This area is known as "Tornado Alley." It is called an alley because it is bounded by the Rocky Mountains to the west and the Appalachians to the east. Tornado Alley covers eighteen states and over 300 tornadoes occur there every year.

Tornado season

In the United States, tornado season runs from February to November, but the peak period is from March to early July. Tornadoes can occur at any time of the day or night, but two-thirds of all tornadoes develop between 2 p.m. and 8 p.m. One-quarter of all tornadoes strike between 4 p.m. and 6 p.m. They are least likely to form around dawn, when the air is most **stable**.

Waterspouts

Waterspouts are like tornadoes, but occur over water instead of land. Fairweather waterspouts occur in calm weather, forming from the water surface up. They are weak, nearly transparent, and last only a few minutes. Tornadic waterspouts are tornadoes over water. They are not transparent and form from the cloud down, occurring while the thunderstorm is still growing.

Landspouts

A landspout is a type of tornado that occurs in most parts of Canada, and on the high plains of Colorado in the United States. Landspouts have a narrow rope-like funnel extending from the cloud base to the ground. They appear under small storms or large cumulus clouds that are still growing. Landspouts are usually weak and short-lived, but they can be dangerous.

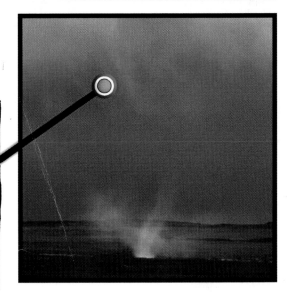

Gustnadoes

Gustnadoes are small whirlwinds that form where downdrafts spill out under a supercell thunderstorm. Gustnadoes spin up a dust cloud at ground level, and are often mistaken for tornadoes. They are weak, but can do minor damage such as breaking tree limbs, overturning garbage cans, and tossing around lawn furniture.

Storm Science

Earth is surrounded by an atmosphere, which is made up of layers of gases. The weight of air in each of the layers puts pressure on the air below it, creating air pressure. When air pressure is high, the day is usually clear and sunny. When air pressure is low, it is cloudy and rainy. When there is high pressure, the air holds more moisture than when there is low pressure. That is why there are fewer clouds on high pressure days.

Latent heat

High in the atmosphere there is less air, so the air pressure is lower. As hot moist air rises, lower air pressure allows it to expand. As air expands, it cools, and some of it **condenses** into water vapor, releasing latent heat into the atmosphere. Latent heat is a form of **energy** that makes the air feel hotter than it is. Cooled air sinks to the ground in a **downdraft** and water vapor stays in the sky, forming patches of fluffy cumulus clouds. The latent heat energy is released into this growing cloud.

Tornadoes can appear different colors. A dark tornado is usually silhouetted in front of brighter skies. A gray, blue, or even white tornado means there is a lot of rain. The tornado will appear the color of the dust it kicks up.

Air movement

As air moves upward, more air is drawn in near the ground to replace it. This happens repeatedly as the air rises and falls, and the amount of water vapor continues to build. The cumulus cloud grows into a lumpy, towering cumulonimbus cloud, or thunderhead. The continual up and down, or vertical, movement of the heated and cooled air speeds up. Hot air rises higher into the atmosphere, until it reaches a ceiling of cold air, called a cap. The cap prevents the cloud from rising any higher.

Anvil cloud

The top of the cloud gets squashed against the cap and begins to spread horizontally, forming an anvil cloud. The cloud is loaded with moisture and energy from the latent heat and grows darker. **Static electricity** also builds as water droplets in the cloud rub against each other. Lightning and thunder begin as the cloud becomes a thunderstorm. If the cloud punches through the cap, the storm grows extremely quickly and becomes far more violent.

A tornadic supercell thunderstorm rotates across central Kansas after dark. A supercell thunderstorm is a good indicator that a tornado is forming. The word "tornado" comes from the Spanish words tornar, which means "to turn," and tronada which means "thunderstorm."

Cumulonimbus clouds

When the movement of air in cumulonimbus clouds becomes very active, the clouds may turn into supercell thunderstorms. At the top of a cumulonimbus cloud is a cap. This is a layer of cooler air that sits above the growing cloud. It acts like a ceiling, keeping the cloud from rising higher in the atmosphere. In a developing thunderstorm, once the cloud hits the cap, the top of it then flattens out into an anvil shape.

Supercell storms

Air travels in masses that are cold or warm, dry or moist. These masses cover huge areas and usually stay separated from each other. An approaching mass of cold air is called a cold front and a mass of warm air is a warm front. There are also gust fronts, which bring very strong winds. These traveling fronts can cause rapid and dramatic changes in the weather in a short period of time, often bringing severe storms.

1 Warm, moist air (red arrows) rises into the cumulonimbus clouds. Air at the top reaches the cloud cap and flattens out into an anvil cloud.

2 If there is rain, the updraft (blue arrows) will be softened. The updraft will hit the ground and fan out into a gust front.

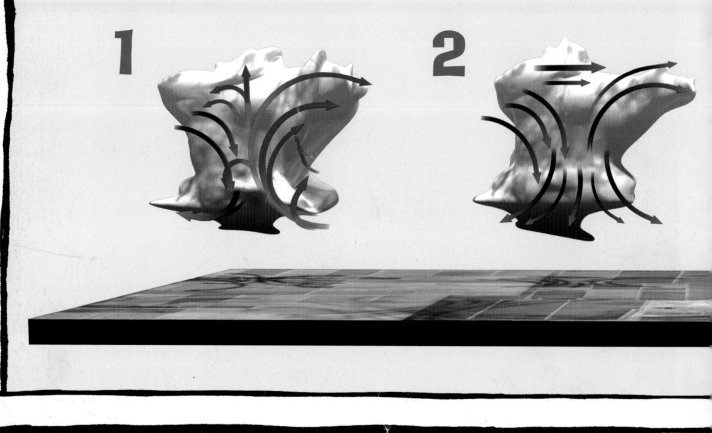

Wind shear

Two masses of air with a stable layer of air between sometimes travel in different directions or at different speeds. If the layer of air at the bottom changes direction, as it does when it heats up and rises, the stable air in the middle is sheared, or cut off, by the rising air. The middle layer starts to roll horizontally like a wheel, pushed in two directions by the winds in the layers above and below it.

Rolling winds

If the rolling air tilts upward into a thunderstorm cloud, it picks up more speed and forms a tornado. In the central part of the United States, the layer of air above the ground is warm, dry, and stable. Cold dry air comes down from northern Canada and slips in above it. Warm moist air from the Gulf of Mexico comes up from the south and slides below it. This forms a sandwich of different air masses.

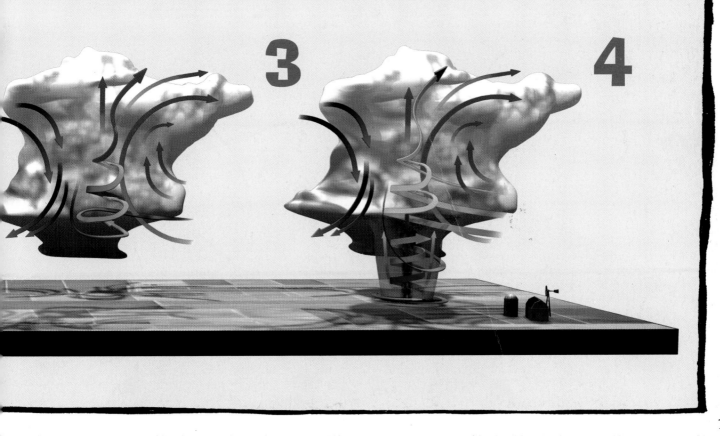

3 Inside a supercell thunderstorm, updrafts (orange arrows) meet in a wall cloud that hovers 1,500 feet (457 meters) above the ground and then spirals upward.

4 As the storm gathers more force, a funnel cloud forms and descends, becoming a tornado when it touches the ground.

Twist and Spout

Tornadoes come in many shapes and sizes. Some are long and narrow from top to bottom like a snake or rope. Others are thick and fat and are called by names such as stovepipe, tube, and cylinder. Tornadoes can also look like cones or wedges, and some even appear like a boiling wall of fog. Inside, all tornadoes operate in the same way.

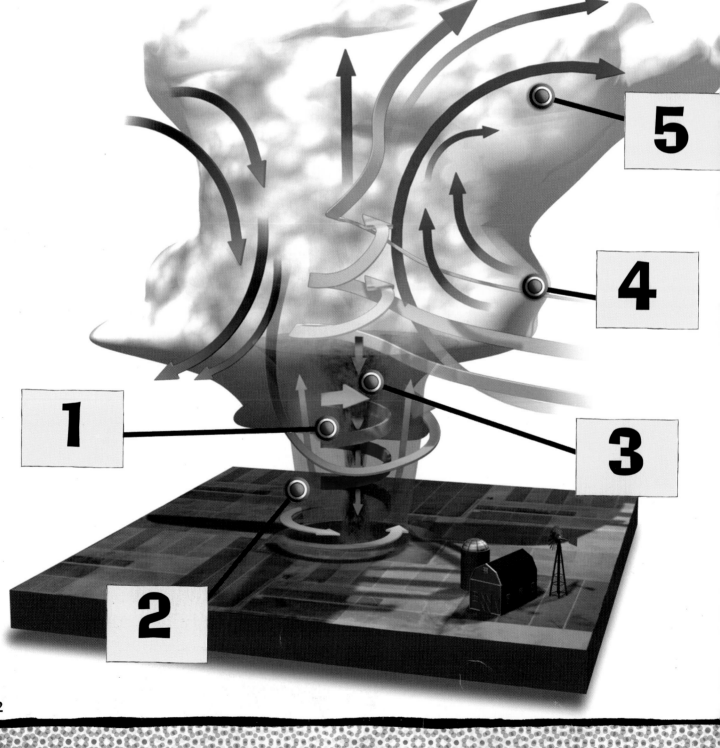

1. Updraft

Warm air (orange arrows) rises in an updraft. As air heats up, it rises with increasing speed, tilting vertically and beginning to spiral, much like water going into a drain upward.

2. Funnel cloud

The funnel cloud is the part of the thunderstorm that spins and stretches down out of the storm cloud. It is not called a tornado until it touches the ground. Around the bottom of a tornado is a debris cloud.

3. Downdraft

The cooled dry air that sinks from the storm cloud (blue arrows) flows quickly out in a downdraft. If the air currents are moving rapidly, the downdraft can exit the storm cloud at great speed. This is called a downburst.

4. Wall cloud

A wall cloud lowers itself from the bottom of the storm cloud just before a tornado develops, or rain or hail begins. If the wall cloud is turning, it means there is rotation in the storm and a tornado may soon form.

5. Cumulonimbus clouds

Cumulonimbus clouds are very tall lumpy clouds. At the top of a cumulonimbus cloud is a cap. This is a layer of cooler air that sits above the growing cloud, which acts like a ceiling, keeping it from rising higher. Once the cloud hits the cap, the top of it flattens and spreads out to an anvil shape. This is a sign that a supercell is forming.

Sea monsters?

Ancient mariners thought that waterspouts were sea monsters. Waterspouts are shaped like long slender tubes or ropes. They move at speeds from ten to fifteen miles per hour (16 to 24 km/h), and usually last for less than fifteen minutes. Some waterspouts have lasted for up to 60 minutes, and packed winds of up to 130 miles per hour (209 km/h). Waterspouts form over warm shallow waters in oceans, seas, bays, lagoons, and lakes, where extremely humid warm air rises and condenses to form clouds. They occur more often in the Florida Keys than anywhere else in the world. In one year, the area can have 400 to 500 waterspouts. Waterspouts can overturn small boats and damage ships.

Thundercloud

Cold air spirals down to water

Warm air sucked up into cloud

Water bulge

Life of a Tornado

In southeastern parts of the United States, tornadoes can come and go within ten minutes. In the central United States, they can last for up to an hour. On average, tornadoes last between five and 30 minutes. The Tri-State tornado of 1925 lasted a record three and half hours!

Fast and furious

The United States has an average of 1,000 tornadoes a year. In countries such as Canada and Australia, many tornadoes strike in **uninhabited** areas where they go unreported. Most tornadoes travel at between ten to twenty miles per hour (16 to 32 km/h), but some have traveled at up to 65 miles per hour (105 km/h).

Unpredictable paths

Tornadoes can move in any direction and change direction without warning. In North America, they usually move from southwest to northeast, or west to east. Tornadoes sometimes change direction mid-path, or double back over ground they have already covered. Some tornadoes stay over one spot, hardly moving at all.

As a tornado gathers force, the funnel cloud descends to the ground. A funnel cloud rotates clockwise in North America. When the funnel cloud reaches the ground it is called a tornado. The debris cloud is made of dirt and dust kicked up by the tornado.

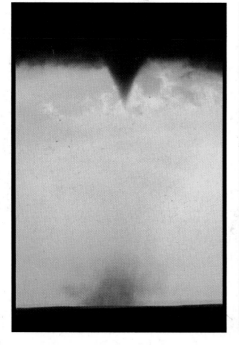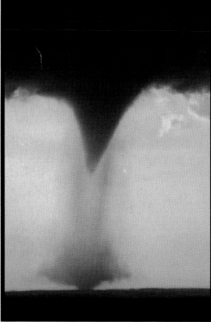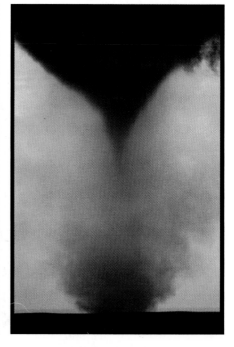

Staying alive

A tornado needs warm, humid air to keep going. If rain begins to fall, cooler air moves down and spreads over the ground, cutting off the tornado's supply of warm moist air. A downdraft from the edge of a thunderstorm can also descend and cut off the warm air supply. When the warm air supply dies, the tornado loses strength and becomes very thin and ropey.

(right) As a waterspout dies, the funnel weakens and becomes shorter and may be more tapered. It often twists around and the bottom may move out from under the cloud.

(below) Before a tornado breaks up and disappears, it often twists wildly, becoming small and thin.

Tornado Alert

From the earliest times, people relied on nature to predict the weather. They noticed that some animals sensed or heard an approaching storm long before people saw it. It was not long ago that people found out a tornado was coming only when they saw or heard it. Today's technology has improved tornado forecasting and saved many lives.

Radar

In the 1970s, it was discovered that the average time between the appearance of a supercell thunderstorm and the touchdown of a tornado was 36 minutes. Researchers realized that Doppler radar helped them forecast tornadoes. By sending out **radio waves** that reflect off water droplets or ice particles, and measuring the returning waves, Doppler radar can determine whether a storm is coming closer or moving away. A nationwide Doppler network in the United States now works so well that people usually have plenty of time to take cover before a storm.

(above) A professional storm chaser videotapes a tornado in Turner County, South Dakota during an outbreak of twisters on June 24, 2003.

NEXRAD

Next Generation Weather Radar (NEXRAD) is another type of radar system that has been installed around the United States. It sends out radio waves from an **antenna**, but this radar works much quicker than the Doppler method. NEXRAD measures the motion of air within storms up to 143 miles (230 km) away. This allows meteorologists to spot signs of developing storms associated with tornadoes more accurately.

Project VORTEX

In 1994, the National Severe Storms Laboratory (NSSL) in the United States ran Project VORTEX, or Verification of the Origins of Rotation in Tornadoes Experiment, to gather the most complete set of observations and measurements of supercells. The scientists studied nine tornadoes and collected a lot of valuable data which they are still analyzing.

(above) Members of project VORTEX prepare to chase tornadoes in Oklahoma, U.S.A.

There are at least 320 meteorological radar systems operating in more than 52 countries. With the use of these radar systems, warning time before a tornado has improved from around four to seven minutes in the 1970s to about 28 minutes in 2003.

TOTO

The Totable Tornado Observatory, or TOTO, was a 400-pound (181-kg) device that researchers hoped to place in the path of a tornado. If they succeeded, TOTO would record the tornado's wind speed, pressure, temperature, and lightning on paper strips. The device was too heavy and difficult to place easily, so it was retired in 1985.

Dillo-cams

Dillo-cams were instruments that were shaped like an armadillo and carried a camcorder inside its **fiberglass** shell. On May 25, 1997, a tornado passed directly over a Dillo-cam. When it was found, the Dillo-cam was battered and dented, but the camera had recorded some spectacular video.

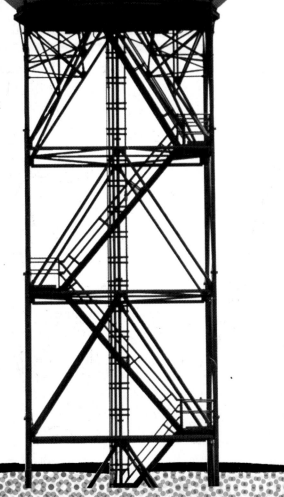

(left) A Doppler radar tower.

(below) TOTO was designed by researchers at the National Severe Storms Laboratory and University of Oklahoma. It was hit by a small tornado only once.

Storm Chasers

Storm chasers are scientists and researchers who work for colleges, universities, or branches of the government, such as the National Severe Storms Laboratories (NSSL). They are trained professionals who can judge the way a tornado is moving and know when and how to keep out of its way. They check data in the morning and look for conditions ideal for severe thunderstorm formation. The information guides them to the general area of the storm. Chasers gather information about storms and try to film, photograph, or take scientific measurements from any tornadoes that occur. They spend a lot of time driving to storms, but may only see a tornado once for every ten to twelve times they chase. If they are lucky enough to see a tornado, they have only a few minutes to unload their equipment, use it, and get out of the way before the tornado gets too close.

Storm chasers in action as winds and rain create a shelf cloud at the edge of a severe thunderstorm in Oklahoma, U.S.A.

Path of Destruction

Tornadoes have been said to shear sheep, pluck chickens, turn an iron jug inside out, and even explode buildings. One was even said to have picked a train off its tracks, turn it around to face the opposite direction, and set it neatly back down on another set of nearby tracks. Of course, all of these stories are false, but tornadoes can do some pretty incredible things.

Pampa, Texas, 2003

Deadly missiles

The high speed of a tornado's winds causes airborne objects to become deadly missiles. The biggest threat to people and animals is from flying debris and from being blown through the air. Flying debris such as corrugated steel roofing, bamboo stakes, iron rods, wood, cooking utensils, and water pots caused most of the deaths and injuries in an October 1997 tornado in Bangladesh.

Winds

A strong tornado can rip up almost anything, even if it appears to be firmly attached. It can uproot huge trees, pull heavy plumbing out of the ground, and tear up roads, fences, railroad ties, and telephone poles. The stronger the tornado, the heavier the things it can carry. In 1931, a tornado caught the Great Northern Railway's express train, The Empire Builder, and toppled five of the 70-ton (64-tonne) coaches off the tracks. It picked up one of the coaches, which was carrying 117 passengers, and hurled it into a ditch 80 feet (24 meters) away. One passenger was killed and 57 others were injured.

Carried away

Really strong tornadoes can rip houses right off their foundations and smash them into a million pieces. In Bangladesh, it does not take a very strong tornado to do that kind of damage. Houses are often made of mud, straw, bamboo, or corrugated steel. Since these structures are quite weak in comparison to brick houses, they are easily demolished by tornadoes. People are sometimes buried alive when their mud and straw houses collapse on top of them. Victims have many wounds caused by the flying metal, and head injuries are the main cause of death after a tornado.

(opposite page, top) In the most severe tornadoes, winds travel at over 310 miles per hour (500 km/h) and can do incredible damage. Weak tornadoes can still tear shingles off roofs of houses.

(above) A child's bicycle wrapped around a tree by a tornado.

(below) Tornadoes will sometimes damage one house while leaving others nearby untouched, such as in this Texas neighborhood.

Hail and lightning

Hail is formed when frozen raindrops repeatedly rise and fall with the wind currents, picking up many layers of ice before being dropped by the storm cloud. Hail can fall right before the tornado hits or just after it has passed. If the hailstones are large enough, they can smash windows in houses and cars, severely damage crops, badly injure people caught outside, and severely damage and dent vehicles. Tornadoes come from supercell thunderstorms, and since those storms are full of energy and static electricity, there is usually a lot of lightning.

(above) Tornadoes can bring large hail, ranging in size from golf balls to grapefruits.

(left) The winds in tornadoes can be strong enough to lift heavy objects, such as this transport truck.

Environmental damage

Tornadoes can severely affect wildlife and their habitats. Living creatures sense approaching storms and quickly take cover. Insects hide in cracks and under leaves. Mice, turtles, frogs, snakes, and lizards move to higher ground to escape drowning in their burrows and holes. Fish go deeper in lakes and streams. Birds stop flying and singing and hide in thick evergreens and shrubs, and large groups of sea birds sit onshore. Waterspouts and tornadoes occasionally pick up large quantities of small fish, frogs, or crabs, and drop them over nearby land. Tornadoes can level huge forests, or strip them of bark, leaves, and branches.

(above) This massive tree was uprooted by a powerful tornado. The woman is holding a tape measuring three feet (0.9 meters) and she is five feet (1.6 meters) tall.

T. Theodore Fujita was a University of Chicago meteorologist who created a scale to classify tornadoes by the damage they had done.

Rating Tornadoes

The Fujita Scale was introduced in 1973 and rates tornadoes from F-0 (weak) to F-5 (violent). An F-0 tornado has 40 to 72 mile per hour (64 to 116 km/h) winds and causes light damage, such as breaking branches, and damaging chimneys and signs. An F-5 is the strongest tornado. Its winds are 261 to 318 miles per hour (420 to 512 km/h) and cause incredible damage, such as lifting houses off their foundations and carrying them for a distance before ripping them apart.

Famous Twisters

The earliest recorded tornado occurred on October 23, 1091. The church at St. Mary le Bow in central London, England, was badly damaged and two men were killed when the church's roof was ripped off. Other tornadoes have caused damage around the world.

Bangladesh

The worst tornado to strike Bangladesh in recent years occurred on April 26, 1989. It cut a long track up to one mile (1.6 km) wide, killed at least 1,300 people, injured 12,000, and left about 80,000 people homeless. It was probably the world's deadliest single tornado.

Australia

In Brisbane, Australia, on November 4, 1973, the most damaging tornado in Australia's history touched down. Its winds were nearly 155 miles per hour (250 km/h), the track, or path, was 31 miles (51 km) long, and the width ranged from 328 to 754 feet (100 to 230 meters). It damaged or destroyed 1,390 buildings and caused over three million dollars in damage.

The Tri-State Tornado of 1925 holds the most records of any tornado in the history of the United States. It caused 695 deaths, traveled 219 miles or 352 km, lasted 3.5 hours, and traveled at a speed of 73 miles per hour (118 km/h).

Tri-State Tornado, 1925

Canada

On July 14, 2000, a tornado hit Green Acres Campground at Pine Lake, Alberta. Eleven people were killed, about 140 injured, 400 campsites were destroyed, and over 60 trailers were thrown into the lake. Damage reports say the winds reached 186 miles per hour (300 km/h) with a 0.6-mile-wide (1-km) path. Baseball-sized hail was also reported.

China

On April 12, 2003, a tornado struck Guangdong Province in South China. It brought hailstones 0.8 inches (2 cm) in **diameter**, cut off electricity and water supplies, caused massive traffic jams by destroying parts of the highway, and caused the flooding of two coal mines and almost 24,711 acres (10,000 hectares) of croplands.

A neighborhood in Moore, Oklahoma, lay in ruins after a tornado flattened many houses and buildings in May 1999. One monstrous funnel cloud skipped across the ground and was classified F-5, with winds of more than 260 mph (418 km/h).

Xenia, Ohio, 1974

(top) On April 3, 1974, a gigantic F-5 tornado tore through Xenia, Ohio. It lasted for nine minutes, killed 33 people, injured 1,600, and damaged or destroyed 1,400 buildings.

Moore, Oklahoma, 1999

Staying Safe

Knowing what to do when a tornado hits can improve your chances of staying safe. If it looks stormy, start taking precautions. Shut all windows and outside doors. Watch the sky from indoors, as weather conditions can change rapidly. Seek shelter immediately if you hear a roaring sound or see a greenish sky, rotating wall cloud, large hail, or blowing debris.

Watches and warnings

When a tornado "watch" is issued, conditions are right for a tornado to form. A tornado "warning" means that a tornado has been spotted. When a warning is issued, go to a shelter immediately and stay there until the danger passes. Listen to a battery-powered radio for weather updates. Severe thunderstorms can produce a lot of rain, so be aware of the potential for flooding.

Taking shelter under a bridge during a tornado is very dangerous. Vehicles can be tossed by tornadoes and people can be killed by flying debris. If you are in a vehicle during a tornado, find a sturdy building and go inside to a windowless area on the lowest level. If no building is nearby, get out of the vehicle, run as far from it as possible, and lie face down flat on the ground in a low spot, such as a ditch, and cover your head and neck with your arms.

Concrete tornado shelters like these ones in Kansas are the safest place to be.

Have a plan

Make a family tornado plan and practice it often. If you do not have a storm shelter, pick a windowless place in the basement that is not below any heavy furniture or appliances. If you do not have a basement or cannot get there in time, find a small windowless room on the lowest floor, such as a closet, bathroom, or hallway. Additional protection from mattresses, pillows, or blankets helps prevent injuries from flying debris.

Emergency kits

Keep an emergency supply kit with enough supplies for three days in your shelter. Each person needs a blanket or sleeping bag, a change of clothing, three gallons (11 liters) of water in airtight containers, and dry or canned food. You also need:

*A first aid kit
*A battery-powered radio
*A flashlight with spare batteries

If anyone uses prescription medicine, include a supply and any special items needed for infants, elderly or disabled people, and pets. Keep everything in easy-to-carry suitcases, duffle bags, or backpacks where they will be quick and easy to grab. Check the contents occasionally, changing the water and food every six months. Make sure batteries and medicines are fresh.

Danger zones

Stay away from windows during a tornado. High winds and flying debris can smash windows. Avoid places like tool sheds containing loose heavy objects, since those objects may become deadly flying missiles. Gymnasiums, large stores, assembly halls, and cafeterias have single-span roofs covered with large sheets of material. Single-span roofs are poorly supported and can easily cave in or be destroyed by tornadoes. Parking lots are also dangerous because cars can become airborne.

Aftermath

Natural disasters such as tornadoes leave lasting impressions on the survivors and the rescue workers who come to help. Each person deals with the event in their own way. Some are able to pick up the pieces, rebuild, and go on with their lives. Others leave the area, while still others live in fear of storms for many years afterward.

Cleanup

In the days before telephones, news of disasters took a long time to reach rescuers. Survivors often had to fend for themselves for days before help arrived. The first help to arrive is usually from friends and neighbors who have survived the storm. They check on the elderly and those living alone, and help dig out people buried under the rubble. Rescue workers use extreme caution when entering damaged buildings, because they may collapse further. They must also watch for fallen power lines and broken gas lines that can cause injuries and fires.

After the Xenia, Ohio tornado, 200 trucks a day rolled through town and it still took over three months to haul away all the debris. The storm took nine minutes to flatten half the town, but it took ten years for the town to recover.

FEMA

If a site is declared a disaster in the United States, relief funds are available to help the community. The Federal Emergency Management Agency (FEMA) is a government agency that deals only with disasters. If an area qualifies for federal disaster assistance, FEMA gives money to help the community rebuild.

Lessons learned

Scientists, **engineers**, and elected officials also visit the area to plan how to prevent similar destruction in the future. These people see what mistakes were made in building construction, and FEMA and the local Emergency Management Agency (EMA) work with city officials to plan construction of safe rooms in damaged public buildings. A safe room is a room capable of withstanding tornado winds. Residents are also encouraged to build safe rooms in their homes.

(above) **This couple and their dog survived a tornado in Benton, Louisiana, by hiding in their bathtub.**

(below) **Organizations such as the Red Cross and the Salvation Army help tornado victims by setting up temporary shelters.**

Recipe for Disaster

Try this experiment to understand how a tornado's spinning winds begin to spiral counterclockwise.

What you need:

*Wide-mouthed clear glass jar (small enough to hold in one hand) and lid

*Colored buttons, beads, or sparkles

What to do:

1. Take the jar and fill it two-thirds of the way with water.

2. Drop in some small colored buttons, beads, or a pinch of sparkles and put the lid on very tightly.

3. Pick up the jar by the lid. With your fingertips holding the jar firmly in front of you, make one quick horizontal circle, keeping your wrist stiff. Now watch your very own tornado in a jar!

4. The sharper you make the circle, the bigger and better the tornado!

What you will see:

The liquid inside the jar forms a vortex, or funnel, that behaves just like a real tornado. The funnel cloud is the part of a thunderstorm that spins, becomes long, and stretches down out of the storm cloud toward the ground. In a tornado, hot air currents rush upward, cool, condense, then sink downward, leaving water vapor behind as clouds. As this up-and-down action speeds up it causes some of the rotating action that results in a tornado.

31

Glossary

antenna A device used to send or receive radio waves

condense To turn from a gas to a liquid

corrugated Made with alternating ridges and grooves

current The path of air in motion

debris The remains of something broken or destroyed

diameter The width across

Doppler radar A device used for finding the location and measuring the speed of distant objects by using reflected radio waves

downdraft The flow of cooled air down out of a thunderstorm

energy A source of usable power

engineer A person who designs buildings, bridges, and roads

fiberglass A material consisting of extremely fine glass fibers that is strong and light

meteorologist A person who studies weather

radio waves Energy waves that carry signals between points without using wires

stable Motionless or very slow moving

static electricity An electric charge generated by friction that builds up on an object

uninhabited Where no people live

Index